When I Muse

CW01425801

Himanshu Dhiman

BookLeaf
Publishing

When I Muse © 2023 Himanshu Dhiman

All rights reserved.

Himanshu Dhiman asserts the moral right to be identified as the author of this work.

Presentation by *BookLeaf Publishing*

Web: www.bookleafpub.com

E-mail: info@bookleafpub.com

ISBN: 9789357741644

First edition 2023

ACKNOWLEDGEMENT

I want to express my gratitude for having a family, around whom I've grown to be so reflective - my parents who are the reason I'm able to sit in the comfort of my chair while I'm writing this, my sisters and brothers-in-law who are the constant source of care and affection in my life, and my cute little nieces who brighten up my world.

I'd also like to thank my school teachers who've instilled the love of writing in me through their language lessons.

And I want to thank my friends and acquaintances who have constantly showered their support and constructive criticism on my blogs and motivated me to keep writing.

PREFACE

Trying not to face a few things again, when I was a kid, I ran so far away that I didn't realize where I had reached. And then I found a piece of blank paper in my hands. The other kids made an airplane out of it, or a small boat. But I did not feel creative that way. So I tried to write. At a time when I couldn't bring myself to connect with people so well, the only way of expressing anything was a blank paper. I poured all my burden onto pages and pages of notebooks and files on my computer. I even started talking - to myself to begin with, and gradually with others.

Sometimes, nobody notices what a child is going through, trying to figure out the meaning of everything that's happening around him and placing every incident into black-and-white. With all the maturity that a child has and everything that he has seen in his life, he might make some decisions related to how he wants to spend his life and what things he wants to tell people. But as he grows up, these things keep coming back to him in challenging ways.

There's no escape from your predispositions or your acquired ways, except that you can write about it on a piece of paper. Sometimes you feel bold enough to show it to a few people. At other times, you publish it online. But there are those times too when you just crumble the paper carrying the weight of your words and throw it away. Nonetheless, it helps.

This is what guides me home. And this is what gives me the motivation to go ahead with this book. You have my pieces of paper now - I can only hope you find yourself in them and draw strength from them.

On My Way to You

You smiled
And I had noticed that for the first time.
It was infectious.
You were infectious.
I couldn't stop that moment
From coming back to my mind in circles.
How could I?
You smiled and it paralyzed me,
I was stuck there for a long time
Trying to look away,
But you didn't stop smiling.

You were upset
And I couldn't ask but I wanted to.
I couldn't understand why the things
That made the world blow around you
Did the same to my world.
You caused the ripples of your sadness
To reach me without having any idea
And I tried to shoo them away,
In a way that was a little too much
And a lot more than required.

You weren't supposed to be
The kind of people I fall for.
I was surprised to discover
That you were probably the one
I was always looking for.
It would have been so perfect.
You would have been so perfect.
I'd have called it serendipity.

But I didn't know the right words to say.
When I'm scared, I struggle with my thoughts.
And my thoughts have always formed a long
chain.
One day, I'll overcome my fears.
Someday, I'll find you.
I'm on my way.

Caged Forever

It's about how confidently
I told myself one day
That I will not let myself fall for you.
It's also about how nervously
I'm telling myself today
That I will get over it.
Till then I'm caged,
Or maybe I'm caged forever.

Though lost in the crowd,
Being quite aware of what's going on around me,
I looked at you.
No, I promise I didn't look at you that day
The way I find myself looking at you now.
Then one day you waved at me
And casually asked me to join in where you
were going.
I said no
And it was still not the time
When I would give a damn about you.
You know that feeling
When you like someone and they don't?
It's this twinge somewhere in your body,
Closer to the heart probably
Because that would make sense.

I felt that.
A million times in one moment
And then in another.
It wasn't the first time but it hadn't happened a
lot.
And even in that small recurrence,
I found myself wishing
To never have to fight myself over it again.

About you,
Maybe I'll just find some respite
In some books or in nature.
I have heard that mountains can talk to you.
I went to one some years ago.
It didn't say much.
It let me momentarily forget someone though.
And then I returned.
A few things had changed around me.
I found myself yet again
Falling for someone so hard.
I woke up one day in my room
To realize that I couldn't stop smiling,
But for how long?
It soon turned into frowns and suspicions.
Foolishly, I thought that at least now
I'm not going to think too much.

Here I am.
Nothing has changed.
One moment, I remember one of you.
And in the other, I just keep trying
To stop the twinges given by the others.

Sometimes, I just stop myself from feeling too guilty
To enjoy the idea of you and I being together.
Sometimes, I think I deserve to not feel any qualms
For being too attentive in life,
Too bothered,
Too much of trying to stay within limits.

I was looking at you in that photograph
Not in the album,
But in my memories.
I couldn't fight myself at that moment.
Like Irma Thomas sang
"The world may think I'm foolish
They can't see you like I can
Oh but anyone
Who knows what love is
Will understand"

What happens when it goes dark?

As we grow up, we wear a lot of emotions on us.
Felicity is naturally everyone's favorite and thus
she's not easy to catch.

It was daytime.
Felicity took my hand and we ran barefoot
Through the sands of the shallow routine of my
life.
Through the water of banters and laughter
We started floating together
And then she left me to take turns with the
others.
You see, she was a lifeguard,
Keeping not just me but everyone else alive.
I kept on swimming further, I had to.
And now it was night keeping me awake with no
whereabouts of her.
What happens when it goes dark?

It was daytime.
Felicity told me that we can jump together from
the sky
As if we were talking about taking a leap into
the water.
I always believed her, so I took a dive
And she dived with me.

She was holding my hand first,
Then she transformed into mist and gusts of
wind, touching my face
And midway she just evaporated
Leaving me a parachute of hope.
I kept on falling further, I had to.
The day had turned into a night again and she
vanished like always.
What happens when it goes dark?

It was daytime.
Felicity just went for a run and I don't know why
I followed her into her madness.
It felt nice to sweat some thoughts out of the
mind
But I couldn't match her stamina.
She maintained her speed, she was a force.
I wasn't and my run turned into a saunter.
And I lost her again.
I couldn't run anymore, although I needed to.
The night still kept me awake and she was
nowhere to be found.
What happens when it goes dark?

It was daytime and it was snowing
And I was wearing multiple rags of pleasure
And Felicity embraced me so tightly that day
That it seemed even the fog can't blur my vision
of her

But then the sun came up from nowhere
Right above us
And she thawed and turned into dew sitting on
the grass
I wasn't going to let her vanish that day.
I dabbed the grass all over. I wanted her
So I tried hard until it started pouring.
Then it rained through the night.
She was with me that night as though she was
not.
Light never fails to show me the way to her, but
What happens when it goes dark?

Standing Out

Today, a shy boy is out on a school trip.
Apparently, he must do that to come out of his
despair
Why would nobody appreciate him taking his
corner
Instead of trying to make space in a crowd
somewhere!

Sometimes, you want to believe your instincts
But people judge your decisions and you attune
And so was the boy thinking of adjusting
Against his inexplicable desire to be a maroon.

Fidgeting his fingers, tapping his legs
He sits in the back of the bus, a typical
wallflower
Avoiding all the eyes, his own crossed with a
reflection
There was another shy kid who needed a bower.

It led to a conversation of stammers and
whatchamacallits.
Inarticulate for some, inept for others.

They didn't need to care about the eloquence,
however.
Completed each other's sentences like they were
brothers.

Serendipity, the first boy said in excitement.
Turned out it's one thing they didn't agree on.
The other kid had gotten himself to understand
That life is not as simple as sitting in a lawn.

To find something or someone you really like
You first need to stop depending on luck
Or expecting someone to bring them to you
Or undermining your strengths like a schmuck

We might be outliers, but not a one-off, he said.
Must learn to stand out 'cause when we do,
Our mettle will battle with their scoff
And our impression on this ground will accrue.

A Letter to The Sea

I stepped a little into your shore that day.
And I realized that there's a magical vibe about you.
It's not strong enough to call me as mountains do,
But when I look at you, I almost want to believe
That even you must be afraid of some things.

How do you contain so much life, so many secrets?
Is it really the moon or your fears pulling that tide?
I like you the best when you do a refrained retreat
And keep taking some of the sand from underneath
my ankle.
That's a form of drowning you trick me into liking.

I stretch my hands and stand at the same spot.
Then I fix my eyes on your waves as if under
hypnosis.
They come towards the shore like a lion approaches
its prey
And then splash me with their roaring supremacy.
Only to return the water to the prerogative sea.

I have been amazed by your powers of mesmerizing,
But I'll always be skeptical of what I can't see
Beneath your not-so-transparent layers of water.
You look pretty and the horizon assures that you do.
But the sun has set and like the night you've become
dark too.

I often come to play a little on the corner of your
shore.
That's up to where my feet trust me to go.
And I definitely like your company at the periphery,
But you're still that friend to me whom I like a lot,
I'm not ready to give myself away to you, however.

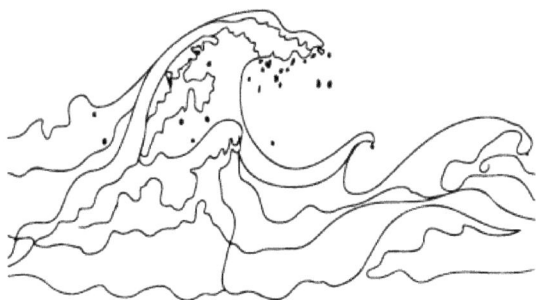

One in a Thousand Kettles

There comes a time when you are tired.
Tired of not how others behave,
As you would like to tell yourself,
But tired of how you react to such behavior!

Sometimes, you express your anger.
Sometimes, you reciprocate with the same
conduct.
At other times, you are wise enough to handle it
with patience.

You feel like a kettle of hope,
Hung from the ceiling of a closed room,
Who considers the room to be its world
And spreading the light within to be its duty,
Made to believe that it's incapable of locomotion
Because the other kettles said so,
As immobile as a paralyzed person in a lucid
dream.

You are aware of the reflections in your reflexes,
Of the frustration showing up on your face,
And of the nearing negativity,
But it takes the conscience of a stable mind,
The forbearance of a wary soul,

And the determination of a heart that can rely on its hunches
To overcome the fear of external control over oneself.

There might be even a hundred people in the closed room
Who do not think, do not judge, do not empathize
Like you do, but that's what makes you better in your eyes
And that's what makes them wiser in theirs.

Multitude is what the world works on,
What teaches you to appreciate the contrasts in life,
What inspires you to become better than someone else.

If you give up to the mere incongruity
Of a thousand thoughts around you,
How will you climb the mountain-like ranges
And stand atop the colossal episode of life?
Or do you not want to?

Waiting for Autumn

You keep knocking on the door of my mind,
And you keep trying to break the windows,
Unwelcomed, unwanted, and unaccommodating,
You keep knocking till I actually open it.
There are some of you who knock from the
outside
Some of you who knock from the inside.
Some wanting to come in from another person
Because you know whom empathy will work on,
Some eager to go outside.
You create such a noise, it makes me deaf
To the thoughts that matter.

You make me shiver in the hottest summer,
Turn me red in the coldest winter,
Make me feel dry even in the abundance of
happiness,
All the water that rained
Trickling down my soul without touching it.
I have my own Autumn season
To shed the leaves which have been there for too
long
And it comes when it comes
I never know how to summon it

But it comes when it comes
And it will come again someday.

Till then, I'll try to hold my door and windows
From the heat and from the frost.
I'll try to let myself feel the rain
And I'll eagerly wait for Autumn

.

Away from the Mainland

To an island where we would be left on our own to
figure out our lives instead of having to go through
the same cycle which others go through, to be able to
build our own unbiased perspective,

Come with me
To that island without access to the loads of
experience that people on the mainland have. Who
uses all of that anyway? People shut their eyes
deliberately to some of it which is beyond their minds
to comprehend.

–

To a meadow where there are doors in the millions of
spaces between the open air and we're free to say
which door we like,

Come with me
To that meadow which is just grass and sky and an
abode to a pristine life waiting for us. All we need to
do is jump through those doors into the kind of world
we want.

–

To a valley of sunlight peeking through the canopies
where we won't have to go through the
uncomfortable conversations with people we love

because the aesthetics inside us would be lost and
mesmerized by all we can see,

Come with me
To that valley so that we can be free of all the clutter
and be at peace with ourselves because there won't be
any distractions from affection but malign, and no
love would ever go unrequited.

–

To a hill where we can be free of frenzied anguish
that the self-proclaimed guardians of conduct of this
mainstream world make us go through,

Come with me
To that hill to leave behind our fears of being
overruled, fettered to the shackles of civilization,
misunderstood, and missed out.

–

Come with me, won't you? I need to find such a
world and I'm not motivated enough to go alone on
the road which leads there;

Because it goes through the world
Of murderers of passion
And abductors of novelty,
Of critics of the unknown,
And snatchers of compassion,
Of those who steal aspirations from our sleeves
And those who speculate and call our actions
unbecoming.

–

To the unbound zenith gleaming all over our heads
with colors during that long-awaited beautiful sunset,

Come with me
To the confluence of integrity and unending love, and
the greatest mirage of all time - the horizon. It is
where the sea, the sky, and the sun go. Surely there
must be something there to pacify us.

A Walk Away from the Soliloquy

Juggling between the comfort of the bed
And the discomfort of his annoying thoughts,
He realized that the sun had set already and finally
His hesitation to go out turned into an urgent need of
getting out.
So he came to a compromise and decided to go for a
long walk
In the brisk gushes of whatever was left of the fresh
air
And in the light of the night hoping to leave the
vileness out on the way back.

A thousand questions popped up again
Forming a chain of conversations with a few people
he knew
And with himself.
The mind would never give it a rest.
The walk always helped though,
It positioned his thoughts in better places than they
were before.
He'd suddenly feel energetic

And all the yearnings would leave the spotty mind.
That's the kind of optimism he was always in pursuit
of.

The room was needed sometimes to rest the body
But his mind?
It was a soliloquy inside his mind.
Voices kept talking until they drove him mad,
They became a monster inside the walls
And turned into a counselor outside them.

A restive spirit always demands a balmy day
And wishes someone could arrest the ruminations
And turn them into reveries.
That might be too optimistic a thought, though.
So his psyche swims away to the offing
In an attempt to rejuvenate.

What a world it would be, he thought,
If he could forget what he didn't want to remember.

Run

There's a life somewhere that you wanted to live,
You have hesitated for so long to create that life
In the place where you have fallen to be.

It feels like you're stuck by these walls all around.
You might not see it but there's a way in and a way
out
To every quandary you've seen or will see in life.

It's not easy to go through something alone,
Never knowing how another person would have
thought
Or reacted to situations that make you feel dizzy.

But you can find more people like you
If you just go to the left or to the right
In this maze of depressions and ecstasies.

Promise yourself that you'll always have hope in your
heart
So that you're strong enough to defend the boundaries
Of your own life and fight your fears with a wide
smile.

There's a life somewhere that you wanted to live,
There's a place somewhere where you wanted to be.
But you can't keep drooling over fantasies.

This is what you have.
And if you want something more or something else,
Break all the shackles,
Take away the enclosures from your line of sight,
Lose yourself, look forward and
Run.

Remember to Conquer with Patience

When you get frustrated by stupidity,
When you feel betrayed,
When things are not going smoothly,
When you can't answer every question that pops
up in your mind,
When you feel like giving up,
When you are facing disappointment from
everywhere,
When you can't sleep properly or even
When you are sleeping too much,
When you're feeling unusually low,
When you are not eating as much as you should
or even
When you're eating much more than usual,
When you don't feel like putting yourself in
other people's shoes anymore,
When you are in turmoil,
Remember that patience has driven you so far,
Remember that your mom always taught you to
trust the fact that good deeds get rewarded
eventually,
Remember that even though overthinking can
leave you perplexed, thoughts are still essential
before making decisions,

Remember to not consider anything as too big of a deal.

It's okay to let yourself feel burdened by all that weight but

Remember to always smile.

Remember to rebel and remember to forgive.

Remember to look at your shadow and get motivated by its nonchalance even in the toughest times when you break down but your shadow doesn't.

And remember to conquer,

Remember to conquer with patience.

Him and Her

It was long after dusk
And a little before dawn.
But he could still see the stars,
Feel the breeze on his skin,
Listen to the sound of the water
Approaching and retreating,
And smell the earth
Splashed with raindrops.

She was in bed.
And the walls of her room came down.
The roof jumped out into the sky.
Everything around
Was getting sucked into a vortex.
She opened her eyes
And started flying too
And that's how her morning began.

The other stars vanished
Under the luster of the one
That came too close
And so he started walking
Towards nowhere.
He was out in the open,
Relaxing and enjoying every bit
Of perpetually changing nature's offerings,
He didn't mind meeting
With surprises on the way.

She was dumbstruck by the force
And furious at nature
For ruthlessly throwing her
Out of her closed walls
For she had planned her full day
Before sleeping the last night
And she couldn't bring herself
To feel fortunate
To have been saved anyway.

It rained a lot that day
And he received every drop
As a dab on his skin,
With his eyes closed but heart open.
Both the star and the clouds
Showered upon him
Seeing such a welcoming gesture
And you know how the seven colors
Painted him at that moment.

It rained a lot that day
And she received every drop
As a slap on her face,
With her eyes open
But heart closed.
Both the star and the clouds
Fled after seeing
Such an unwelcoming gesture
And you know how the darkness
Tainted her at that moment
And the moments to come later.

If You Could Read My Thoughts

My cheeks flushed and ears turned red.
I felt overwhelmed by the way my body was reacting.
My feelings shot up to hit my head
All the way to my mouth to voice those thoughts.

But then there was a recoil right back in the heart.
I was scared too, of how you would react.
Every day since then I've come a little closer
To telling you something about myself.

Some things about me, some things about you too.
Some love that I desire, some love that I require.
Every time I try to tell but then decide not to
I kill an emotion growing inside me.

Sometimes, it feels like a usual thing to do.
Sometimes, it becomes an ordeal
And I just remind myself of a thousand things
Out there which require more attention.

So here I am standing in front of you,
Speaking to you on the phone, texting you,
Either falling for you in every next second
Or falling behind somewhere in my life.

And I want you to know, even though I can't decide
If it's the right time to tell you this or if it will ever
be,
That I feel like I won't be able to do this alone
anymore
But I've decided to not let an unrequited affection
overpower me.

Ma

Ma, I had a dream last night.
I was a kid and you were walking me through the streets.
I didn't let you get away from me for even a second
But then you dropped me at a place with another caretaker.
Why didn't you look back at me? I was crying so hard.

Ma, time passed and I got used to that place with other kids.
You took me back home every day and I was happy to get into the comfort of home.
I grew up.
You didn't let me get away from you for even a second.
Time passed and I wanted to go to another place.
So you said your goodbyes and I failed to notice that you were crying.

Ma, it was such a vivid dream.
You became older and I entered my youth.
I had a very different life where I kept running

Without a thought about myself,
Without a thought about you and Papa.

Even in a dream, I felt such agony and agitation, Ma!
It seemed like a sacrifice that I was making
Without even realizing that it was a huge compromise
For expectations to remain unfulfilled,
Giving up all the energy that I got from all the care
you provided me,
Dragging along the weight of disappointments.

Ma, can you make sure I don't sleep today?
I don't want to dream about it again.
Why would someone want to have that life?
Is that going to happen when I grow up?

Ma, please stay by my side tonight.
Please stay by my side and stop time, if you can.

Ma, will I forget you like that someday?
Ma, I'm sorry if I do.

An Insignificant Phoenix

*We often excuse ourselves from picking something up
or taking a new step in the quest for perfection. But
what we forget is that it's not always in our destiny to
complete something that we started, or be perfect at
it. And not being able to complete a hundred percent
of something should not be deemed a failure. It's a
stepping stone, a hand that is helping push the next
person to the place where it ended for us.*

There were a billion stars, but ten of us in this fuss.
Colossal and celestial them, and insignificant us.
Every night, a phoenix rose from the ashes
Of suppressed wants, and emotional crashes.
Pristine was its form, but 'One' ignored its power.
'Two' was fierce, but stormy was its shower.
Flightless but ferocious, 'Three' opened the door
For the 'fourth' phoenix, to get inspired by its lore.
A conundrum in the mind, that was the life of 'Five'.
'Six', however, was focused and prepared for the dive,
An impossible feat, to bring 'Seven' into this world,
Who evolved into 'Eight', buoyant and curled.
Then arose 'Nine' one night, and broke the spell.
The same night saw 'Ten' gushing out of its shell.
A billion stars, in the night sky, exploded with zest.
Out we came, one by one, of our unsettling nest.
Ten fell before us, until we learnt how to fly
Ten fell before them, to learn to look at the sky.
Ten will fall again, but we have come so far,

One of us will aspire and another will become a star.
We don't know if any of us is the special 'one'
But if we don't try, how will we unveil the Sun?
So we won't ever stop, or ever take pride
In our insignificant milestones of a significant stride.
There were a billion stars, only ten of us, however.
Insignificant before celestial, but glistening forever.

Sophie's choice

Holding on to something that you like is a habit
not easy to leave behind.
Some of mine are paving my way to something I
deeply desire,
But there's a fear that if I jump the signal I'm
looking at,
The earth behind it will fall off and stop existing.
I can only go forward from there, whichever
way forward is.

Forward
. Forward
.. Forward
... As if that matters.

There is a deeper sense, however, of what could
lie ahead.
It could be the greenest pastures to begin with
And then a hill or more difficult to climb,
Which should be tolerable given how good the
start would be.
Or it could be the hot dunes
Where I will lose my breath sometimes in
pursuit of an oasis.

But.
But..
But...
Whatever traces I have for whatever/whomever I
like -
They swirl in a whirl like the fallen leaves would
do
When they're touched by a storm.
Meanwhile, I'm sitting in my room,
Unaware of what's going on behind the walls
And the signs of the storm would make me feel
amazing
On account of the pleasant weather that it
follows,
Until it shakes me and I take a big leap and fall.
Follows the inability to sleep due to restlessness.

Left, right, up, down,
here's a thought, here's another,
ceiling, words, memories, wanderings,
left, right, here's a thought,
it's cold, it's hot, it's uncertain
until
it's also dark!

A whole world inside, a whole world outside.
The earth behind does fall off for those who
choose the inner one.

Momentary desires - when they come back
After weeks, months, or years, or through a
trigger -
They make you weak and you can decide then
Either to hit them back aggressively
So that it's not possible for them to bounce back,
Or you can let them consume you.
Until then, your heart will be stuck in a loop
like a broken cassette player singing over and
over,

What I have,
is that too precious to lose
for
what I would like to have?

You've Got This

There is a messenger of darkness
Waiting outside my door
Knock knock knock knock
Knock knock it goes on
The temptation is too strong!

There is also a packet of hope,
A bit shy, so it's hopping but also hiding
It tries to call me towards itself
It says, "You've got this.
You've got this. You've got this."

I pull my hands out of my pockets
And extend them toward the hope
When darkness is all around me
Telling me to give up and be morose.

There's weakness, impatience, and doubt
Emanating strongly from the door
But the little packet is confident enough
That I need not be afraid of them anymore.

So I repeat this to myself like a chant
"You've got this. You've got this.
You've got this."
And I close my eyes, then wake up,
To find that the door has been dismissed.

Chunks of Yearning

I had no idea that it was coming my way.
Nestled in the happy phases of my childhood,
Ignorant of the implied intentions of people's acts,
I sensed an excitement in the form of goosebumps.

A curious mind, now more curious than ever,
Wired to and driven by the heart,
Selected things it wanted to be curious about.
Some of these quenched my fascination,
While some threw me back with apathy.

Some, however, met me midway,
And manifested as a fear of an unrequited affinity.
Every time I hit the wall of this fear,
It ricocheted me off itself,
Splintering my spirit into vulnerabilities,
Leaving the chunks of yearning
Scampering on the ground.

There are some things out there
Which do this to me -
Hit me like a breeze
Calming me down at that moment,
Frolicking my whole within in the next
And causing my blood to bob up and down.

In my heart, in my dreams,
There is a world without rules and precursors.
Everyone is born anew
And no one turns a blind eye to instincts.
Imagine if you could do whatever you felt was right
Instead of what was perceived to be!

I haven't had the courage to pick those chunks up yet
Out of the fear that they might fall again,
Out of the fear that they might just be lying there
As pronounced evidence that everything I have done,
Every path I have decided to step on was wrong
And every path that was my almost will turn into a
regret.

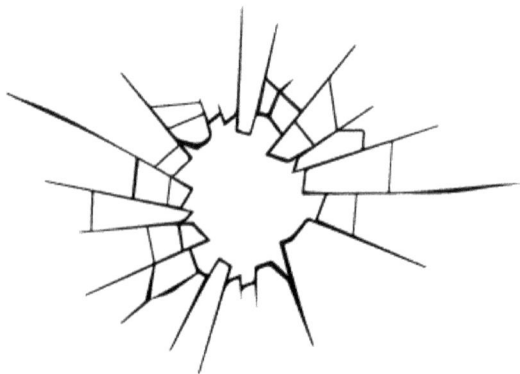

When Stress Knocks on My Door

When stress knocks on my door,
I collect a bit of it,
And throw it down to the bottom of my mind,
Then deal with the rest which falls in my instant
capacity.
It comes and goes like that,
Giving me a semblance of everything being all right!
While I'm distracted by the humdrum of the day,
It piles up, however.
You know what happens then!

When stress knocks on my door,
I feel that as a grown-up I should be able to handle it.
That feeling fills me with disappointment and
helplessness,
And they are good friends with stress.
So it only makes things worse.

When stress knocks on my door,
Food appears to keep me at bay,
Workouts seem to keep me engaged,
But sometimes,
Every moment I enjoy is filled with guilt.
Sleep doesn't come easy,
And eyes get puffy.
Cells die prematurely,

But that knowledge doesn't stop me from falling into
the ditch.

When stress knocks on my door,
Running away from it
Or shunning it doesn't favor me.
Introspections and conversations about it can be
uncomfortable and awkward,
But until I identify and acknowledge the source,
It's not going to go away.
So while I'm gazing at the walls or the open sky,
I might as well dig out the diary I buried long ago,
And start talking to it about our dear friend.

Quarter-Life Crisis

My eyes would blink and close up every now and then but something still doesn't let me sleep. And so I welcome to my mind a new shape of the old dilemma today. A part of me wants to be challenging and yearns to discover, but another part doubles down on me and makes me trust myself a little less every day.

Yes, you are in your late 20s,
I know it's scary.
It feels as if there's so much more to be done,
It also feels as if so much is slipping away,
One day you were on the promenade -
Carefree, dumping worries on the future you,
You slept for a while,
And now you find yourself in this backyard
With the same old wall of rusty tin,
The sky, the sun, the clouds
Have all lost a bit of their color,
It's gloomy all around.
The future has arrived and with it,
The pacts that you have been making with it,
You don't have a clue of how and where to trod!

You want something, you do!
You know that you know what it is,
But you hide your needs,
Shame them by the name of desires,
And then throw them on the road.

*My eyes blinked again and a part of me wants to
sleep so that I wake up in peace tomorrow! But a
part of me worries, turning a sliver here and
there grey!*

Sometimes my restless heart
troubles my eyes and my hair this way,
And there's nothing in the world
That can still seize the day
Like acceptance can!
I don't know the answers to all my problems
today,
but if I've brought them till here,
The shore can't be that far away!

So I can call it whatever I want - quarter-life
crisis or late 20s crisis, but who am I kidding?
When has life ever seemed perfect to me?

Perfection has always been hidden in hindsight
and future prospects.

*...and somewhere between that hell of a spiral
and the radio pumping my ears, my eyes finally
got their way!*

Truth

Locking it in my mind,
In hindsight, I was blind,
The truth always seemed so given!
It came with its pain
Which knew no restrain
And yet I let myself be driven.

Here I was nicely sitting,
Never pausing, always thinking
That someday I will wear it out!
But I'd end up teary-eyed,
Always wondering how to hide,
This shameless and involuntary bout!

A day then came by
I thought this would be why
Everyone talks about being patient.
I chanced upon something,
So sought after, but so numbing.
That day the hard truth became ancient.

A new doubt was born,
My reality was torn,
How could I have not seen it coming?
I panicked of course,
Kicked out of my course,
It seems I am lost and always running!

Unrelatable

I was that piece of the first impression of a meeting
That was thrown out because you decided
To cool down and not be so harshly authentic.
What was it about expressing yourself inside out
That repulsed others so much
When they wished to do the exact same thing
Subconsciously or even while daydreaming?
What was it about authenticity
That it didn't matter so much
As the validation did
In the eyes of the society?

I wish I had a reset button for tailoring myself
To the likes and demands of this world,
But I fail to align myself to that path, repeatedly.
Sometimes I try to cross this ditch
Between my desires for myself
And my desire to be a part of the world,
But it might be that this distance
Is not convincing enough to make me fall in line
With what you think.
It troubles me when I can't find people
Who can relate to this thought,
But why did my heart grow this way
That I had to look for other souls
Searching for the same thing as me?

I hear you
That I am not behaving
Like other people would in my shoes,
But if you told me
That today was the day of the apocalypse,
You would be surprised by
The unfinished things that I would cry over.
And that's how our lives are -
Unrelatable maybe,
But unusually unadmittedly satisfactory.

I am awake troubled by the craziest things
That you could ever imagine
But not stirred a bit by the things
That might rock someone else's world
If they were in my position.
I sleep in my own world of carelessness,
Which I hope all of you do.

Should I aspire to wake up
To your side of the world someday?

Grown-ups

There is a thought in my mind
That has found its way to my heart
(Or is it the other way round?)
It feels like something -
A gesture, a word, a presence -
Has touched me in a way
That makes me feel
Like I need to reciprocate it to you.
But the thing is that if I let this idea
Leave my body and hit the air,
You might think of me as vulnerable.
And I have no idea why I care about that
(Maybe because I've seen others do it too).
I wish the thought was heavier
Than the gulp in my throat
That has taken it down.

Sometimes, I feel that
You want to spend more time with people too,
But what is it that's convincing all of us
To be more reserved as we grow?

I think we underestimate the power
Of sitting together and
Letting those crazy ideas out of our heads,
Without any music in the background,

Without any of those games
That are usually played with the intention
To break the ice or pass the time.

We underestimate our conversations
And the silence that passes between them.

What if we keep growing up
Without losing these precious things in life
That we have gathered
Out of a touch of carelessness in our youth?

Willpower

I swivel around the core that defines me,
That asks me why I feel the way I feel
That wants to believe in something very strongly
But neither here nor there does it think it would
settle.
Throughout the day, I read and I see,
And for those few hours, I'm on the line.
Then I also think and I can't stop but feel too.
And that takes me back to wherever it is I usually am.

Sometimes, you have to force yourself out of the bed,
Out of where you lie in comfort,
Running away from your battles,
You have to put your feet on the ground
And walk no matter how much it pains
Because nobody else can fight on your behalf.

On some mornings, you might decide to rest
But no amount of rest will be good enough
So, look at that ground and move.
Don't build your world around this bed of lies,
Around wherever it is you like
Because what you like isn't necessarily what's good
for you
So don't try to settle till you feel unsettled.

There's a long road ahead.
It might have been troubling so far
And make no assumptions
It will be more troubling further ahead
But if it's hard for you,
Know that those troubles chose you
Because they would build you bit by bit
And complete whatever you think you're missing!

So, walk!
Walk till the effort to walk goes unnoticed by you.

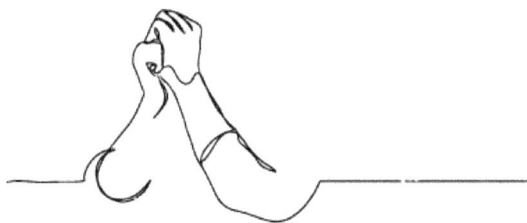

Believe

The scene your mind creates when you're lost
listening to an energizing song,

The little things in other people which intimidate
you,

The decisions which make you have second
thoughts before you hit the send button on them,

The things which you find yourself talking about
the most,

The talents which someone appreciates in you,

The "Oh, I wish" moments which you take
lightly,

The "I'm working on this" struggles which are
hard enough to make you take steps back,

They're all real. If they can exist as a thought in
your mind, they can exist outside it as well. You
just need to let them take you away!

Believe.

Was it love?

"Naive and feeling close to a person
For the first time,
I listened to you and
Believed every word that came out.
Sitting there, so emotionally dumb,
I let you hug me,
A pain inflicted by someone,
Healed by someone else."

"I like you but I don't know
How to articulate that to you,
So when I saw you breaking down,
I did what felt natural,
Showed you my support
By putting my arms around you,
No words were said that day,
But I told you a lot,
I really did."

"Can I ask you something?
I know I'm in my own head
Imagining how perfect things could be
And I'm getting hurt
By my own failure to manifest that.
How did I end up
Falling for someone like that?"

"You're scared
But it's going to turn out fine.
I'm scared too of admitting
What's going on inside me.
I think I love you
But it could be the rush talking.
It could also be that I really do.
I probably shouldn't have said.
But I'm also scared that
It might anyway
Become apparent someday."

"The ride is about to go higher
And you chose this moment
To bring this up?
You admit your feelings today
But you will forget all about it tomorrow
And what my words
Aren't able to express today
Will be expressed a thousand times
In my behaviour tomorrow
And you will vanish some day
Like this never happened."

"You're right
And that's why I hesitated
Even though I have affection
For you in my heart,
I don't know
If my place is with you.
By telling you, I'm sorry
If I caused you to fall for another
I probably won't be able
To love you like you want me to.
I have to deal with my own pain
And you have to deal with yours!
We both will hopefully find love in others."

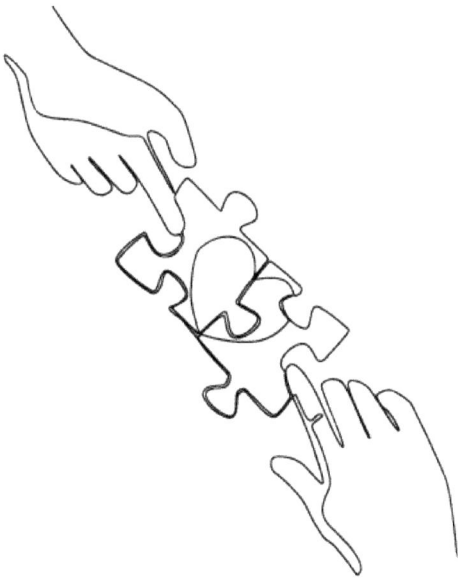

Infatuation

I was walking in a crowd and you were there too.
Did I catch your eye while I bent to fix my shoe?
You had a vibe, that made me stand still on the spot,
And I was, in fact, on the verge of being caught.

I looked at you from the corner of my eyes
Then turned them up as if looking at a million skies
When you looked in my direction all of a sudden
And I pretended to be responding to a summon.

Then you vanished in the crowd, I disappeared too.
Now looking back at that memory is all I can do.
A question that I had then, still lingers in my mind,
If I had smiled at you, could our hearts have aligned?

You won't drown

Like the gushes of winds with some grains of sand
It comes in heavy but it ain't all that grand.
It lights up a fire that is tough to control
But there isn't a flame that you can't withhold.

Don't you lose hope if it takes you down
You've got to cope, I promise you won't drown.

At the beach, the ocean's might is all you see,
Every other thing then fails to be.
The sky looms over your little presence
But you forget that the moon also crescents,
The mighty sun also goes down
And billions of other faces also frown.

Don't you fret, come out of your enigma
It's not a threat, you don't have any stigma.

You heed it and the cloud will naturally grow
You tell it to go elsewhere to put on a show!
The sky goes dark before it turns into rain
but then it also loses its mighty high reign.
Snap your fingers, it's time to come out
Believe me, the cloud won't survive your clout!

The Stinging Sweater

Weighing on my shoulder,
Heaving on my chest,
Why do you love me so much
My boulder of unrest!

You glimmer in the winter
And shrivel when you wish.
We tend to play a long hard game
Where I linger and you dish.

Soaking in that lather,
You crumbled on that day,
But then you came back to me
Only to put me at bay.

Rocking in my chair,
Sitting by the window,
I can feel the wind on me.
You've also settled in though!

Your embrace is so firm,
What do I do but cry?
I sometimes cannot bear you
'cause that's how much you pry.

You form a snuggly fabric
That I want to ignore,
A creature of disorder
Whom I cannot adore.

You little ball of wool,
Bobbing by its strings,
Scheming to be a sweater
That pinches me and stings!

Chasing Felicity

A few pages back, I introduced you to my friend
Felicity and I told you how I keep losing her out
of my sight.

Even though it was difficult to keep track of her,
Those were good times.
But now, we haven't met in a while.
Maybe, she has changed her looks
And I can't recognize her anymore.

I try to find her in every person I meet,
Familiar or unfamiliar.

I chased her till the whole 2 minutes of sunset
And the whole 2 minutes of sunrise
But I seemed to just make a fool of myself.

Was she a physical entity in my life
Or was she just a concept?
I now feel like I can't relate to the feeling of
being attached anymore
But maybe it's all a trap.

Maybe, I'm not welcome in her world.
Maybe, I am and I don't realize
So, I overreact.

Felicity, I almost feel like I'm close to you
But the peer pressure meddles with my mind,
And I don't want to blame the rest of the world
for this,
So let me take some blame for this whole thing
myself.

I don't know how to find you.
And even if I can,
I don't know how to keep you,
So can you knock on my door
And pat me on my head,
And startle me to come out
Of this meaningless quest?

You do knock some sense out of me
When I look at the world around me
And see the real pain lingering everywhere.
I am aware of how better off I am
When compared to the majority
Of unlucky people in this world.
But I forget
And I keep forgetting
That it's a privilege
To be able to feel
And take some time out to ponder
To be able to smile
And take some time out to laugh

To be able to see
And take some time out to observe
To be able to walk
And take some time out to run towards my
dreams.

But all my life, I have been asking myself
"What are you?"
Or rather "Who are you?".
I'm wasting my life chasing you,
And you know that, don't you?

When Courage Meets Convenience

I blinked my eyes
And all those troubles were gone,
But something inside of me was gone too.

It takes a lot of love and affection
To turn yourself away from what you want
And surrender to what life can provide you.
And love and affection I have plenty.

It takes only a pinch of courage, however,
To take that step
Toward your own happiness and sanity.
And it's only when
You're at your best from the inside
That you can do your best
At helping the world.

It's only when you have healed
That you can heal others.

In the conflict with convenience,
Let courage shine for a change!

Milton Keynes UK
Ingram Content Group UK Ltd.
UKHW020740291223
435170UK00015B/643

9 789357 741644